Mark Oman

the 9 Commandments of GOLF

...According to
The Pro Upstairs

Illustrations by Doug Goodwin

COSMIC SECRETS FOR MASTERING THE GAME!

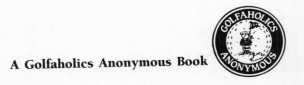

A Golfaholics Anonymous Book

Published by Golfaholics Anonymous®
P.O. Box 222357
Carmel, Ca 93922

Library of Congress Catalog Number: 88-81603
International Standard Book Number: 0-917346-07-6

Printed in the United States of America

This book is dedicated to golf...

The glory and the grief
The small triumphs and the
great humiliations

The light-hearted camaraderie
on the first tee
The heartbroken remorse
at the 19th hole

The unchaste and bitter and awkward
The pure and sweet and natural

The dream of tomorrow's perfection
The nightmare of yesterday's disaster

The profanity
And the prayers

Simply all the things that make
the game worth playing

'Golf's the elixer of youth! You can be a kid again. Wear funny clothes and hats. Play with your own bag of toys. And then you can laugh at your own damn foolishness. And that's the healthiest thing of all! Because laughter jiggles your guts. Tickles your insides... Laughter is the catalyst for great expectations!'

The Pro Upstairs

CONTENTS

Prologue

PART I

Christmas Eve, 1985
Carmel, California

PART II

The 9 Commandments

Epilogue

Prologue

With few exceptions, the true nature of the game of golf has long been shrouded in mystery. I hope what follows may help to change that.

The story you are about to read I had held inside for two years. It just wasn't the kind of thing you go around talking about. Let me say right here that there is no doubt in my mind that the fantastic events recounted here, did in fact, actually happen to me on that fateful Christmas Eve in 1985.

Given the current interest in and growing acceptance of such metaphysical happenings as spirit guides from another plane channeling information through physical beings on this Earth plane, the following may not seem all that outrageous to some of you.

However, for most of you I suspect we will be navigating through uncharted, twilight zone waters. Frankly, some of you may not be ready for these cosmic revelations. In fact, I fully expect there to be many of you who will shortly be muttering, "This guy isn't playing with a full set of clubs. Needs to have his headcovers examined!"

All of which may be true. It hasn't been easy, even for me. After 30 years of playing the game one way, it wasn't easy for me to change the way I thought about golf and played it. My whole personal relationship with the game was called into question.

And now yours is about to be.

I'm sure you've noticed that the subtitle of this book is **Cosmic Secrets for Mastering The Game.** How easily we forget that golf is a game. To be played. Which is fortunate since we are never going to beat it. All the great golfers discovered at some point in their careers that they were never going to beat golf so they better learn how to master 'the game of golf.'

As for the 'Cosmic Secrets'? Well, even The Pro Upstairs finally admitted to me that these 'secrets' have been around for thousands of years, only to have gotten lost in the rough along the way.

Well, it's time to cut the rough, move out of the dark ages and into the age of enlightenment! Or as Bobby Jones said, "Golf is played mainly on a five-and-a-half inch course — the space between your ears."

That is what this book is all about.

I think you will discover, as I did, that what makes these Commandments so valuable is that they are within the grasp of everyone who plays the game. Anyone can put them to use. You don't have to be a scratch player to get the most out of these secrets. You just have to have the itch to play this game as you have never played it before — that is, to the best of your abilities rather than the worst; to enjoy each and every round of golf as if it were the last golf you would ever play.

Think you're ready?

Then send your doubting mind to camp, dial direct to your higher self, put trust in your gut, turn the page and get ready to discover...

The 9 Commandments Of Golf... According To The Pro Upstairs.

"If this was what golf was like in heaven, I was ready to ask for a starting time."

PART I

Christmas Eve, 1985
Carmel Valley, California

The Pro Upstairs

"AHHHHHHHHHHHHG..."

I cringed and raised my eyes to the cruel heavens. Looking back down didn't change anything. The ball was still six inches short and left of the hole. How could I yank it so bad? It was an easy two-foot putt straight up the hill.

I had just made a tough 15-footer on the 10th hole to save par and now to blow this easy one on the 11th made me angry. "Nice Christmas present," I muttered to myself and slapped the ball off the green with my putter.

Still cranky, I grumbled some un-holiday spirited thoughts about the infernal game, slammed the putter down into my bag, slung the thing over my shoulder and trudged to the 12th tee.

The back nine on the West Course of Rancho Canada in Carmel Valley, California is not particularly long even from the blue tees — which is the only way to play it when your ego refuses to accept your handicap. The holes hopscotch back and forth across the Carmel River and many of the fairways are tight corridors through thick patches of cottonwoods and sycamores.

Long before this was a golf course, the area was part of a land grant given to Lazaro Soto by the Mexican government. The golf course today retains a certain romantic old world comfort about it.

Sheltered on the south by the rugged Santa Lucia Mountains, the back nine can be heaven on earth late in the afternoon, with the afterglow of the sun sending splashes of color through the trees and dancing shadows across the fairways — which is why I usually like to play a few holes at this time of day. If I time it right, there may be only half a dozen players on the whole back nine.

That night there were none. I was it. The fact that it was Christmas Eve may have had something to do with it. I guess most people had more important places to be and things to do. In truth, so did I, but it didn't stop me from getting out to play. The air was cool and crisp. The sky was clear. The course was mine alone to walk upon and worship.

All of this was on my mind — until I yanked that two-foot gimme on eleven.

Now I was upset. I stood on the 12th tee glaring hard down the narrow fairway. It was a short par-five, about 470 yards, but the landing area was extremely tight, with thick patches of tall trees on either side to grab all but the most perfectly placed drive. A low, screaming 2-iron down the pipe is the correct shot. So naturally I took out my driver. I set up to the right of the tee, aimed slightly left and was going to cut it ever so slightly left to right with the ball ending up 240 yards down the right center.

I swung, put a nice over-the-top right shoulder into it and hit a left-to-left duck hook.

"Son of a bitch..."

I whirled around, reared back and threw my driver as high and far as I could. I watched as it sailed up and into a clump of trees behind the tee.

Did *I* just do that?? I hadn't thrown a club since I was a kid. We're talking 30 years ago. What came over me? It was almost as if I had

13

> **'** *... there was a horrible CRACK! and a flash almost like lightning... When I looked back, my driver was flying out of the tree and heading straight for me!* **'**

no control over it. Flip Wilson immediately popped into my head. "The devil made me do it. Made me hook it and throw the club. Couldn't have been *me*!"

Well, at least no one saw me do it. I was grateful for that.

All of this went through my mind in a second — about the time it took my precious 1960 Eye-O-Matic MacGregor Tourney persimmon classic to sail through the air and disappear into the branches of the tree.

Silence.

I listened for the club to rattle around in the branches and fall down to the ground so I could forgive and forget.

Except there was no rattling. Nothing. Being December most of the leaves had fallen from the trees. Being California there was still enough foliage that I couldn't see my club.

The world was perfectly still and quiet. My priceless MT driver had stuck up in the tree.

"God-damned game..."

The words were barely in the air when the branches of the tree began to shake and moan as if God Himself had His hands around the tree's throat and was shaking the hell out of it!

All of a sudden there was a horrible CRACK! and a flash almost like lightning. I turned away. When I looked back, my driver was flying out of the tree and heading straight for me!

I couldn't move.

WHAP!

I was nailed dead solid perfect between the eyes with my own Eye-O-Matic MT Driver.

I don't know how long I was out, but it was nearly dark when I regained semi-consciousness. (I say semi-consciousness because what happened next, to this day, doesn't seem real. And yet it must have happened. There is no other reasonable explanation for the events that followed.)

It was a voice that first aroused me from my K.O.

"Sorry about that, Sport. But you asked for it."

My eyes opened to a pair of shoes a few inches in front of my face. Actually they weren't exactly shoes. More like sandals. Very old sandals. The kind with lacings crisscrossing around the foot and ankle and up the leg. You know, the type of thing Charlton Heston wore in *The Ten Commandments*. Except these sandals had golf spikes on the bottom.

My gaze traveled up the figure before me, which was outfitted in an old pair of rather seedy-looking knickers. A rope tied around the waist was holding the whole thing up.

"You know, I've always wanted to do that. Just wasn't the right time or place. Until now..." said the voice.

"Whaaaa..." I lifted my head and tried to focus in on the face that went with the voice.

"I guess it was just your lucky day, Sport." The face smiled and bounced its eyebrows. The eyebrow bounce reminded me of Tom Selleck on *Magnum P.I.* But the face reminded me of a sporty Albert Einstein. An unnerving combination.

I closed my eyes and was trying to clear my head when the voice said, "Say the secret word and you win a playing lesson from The Pro Upstairs!"

My eyes popped open. "What...Who *are* you?"

"I just told you, The Pro Upstairs. Can't you tell?"

He had a point. It was written all over him. This guy was ready for the tour. On his sweater vest there was a big white puffy cloud emblem. Inside the cloud was the scripture, The Pro Upstairs, in gold.

But his Hogan-style cap was really eerie. It wasn't exactly on his head, but more like hovering over it... like a halo.

The cloud on the front of the visor wasn't embroidered either, but

> *'I must be dead. That's it. This is God's way of telling me to forget the back nine.'*

floated free from the headband. And The Pro Upstairs scripture inside the cloud sent out sparkles of gold dust.

"Holy shit!" I thought. "I must be dead. That's it. This is God's way of telling me to forget the back nine." The inside of my head felt like a couple of guys slinging sledgehammers into the last spike of the transcontinental railroad.

"No, you're not dead, Sport," said the voice. "But you are right about one thing. He **is** trying to tell you something. Why do you think I beamed you in the head with your own driver? Had to get your attention somehow."

"Are you telling me...**you** are God?"

"Do I look like George Burns?"

"I must be going crazy..."

"You surprise me, Sport. I really didn't think you'd take it like this. I figured you'd get right into the spirit of things. I mean, this is the age of enlightenment — cosmic consciousness!"

"Yeah, right..."

"What's the matter with you? Haven't you read Shirley MacLaine??? You know, entities from the spirit world. Good stuff from the astral plane? Where have you been, Sport — on another planet?"

"Where have **I** been! Where have **you** been?! You tell me you're The Pro Upstairs and expect me to believe you're from some sort of... I don't know... golf heaven?"

"Look, I know this isn't easy for you, Sport. It's never easy being the first salmon to reach the top of the stream."

"What are you talking about?"

"And you don't really believe there's such a place as golf heaven, do you?"

"Me? **You're** the one who —"

"Believe me, it's the same up where I come from as it is down here. Well, almost."

"Say the secret word and you win a playing lesson from The Pro Upstairs!"

> **' You think God hits the ball any better than you do? '**

"Wait a minute. Just hold it a second. Are you saying golf is just as hard...up there...as it is down here?"

"Hell, yes! You think God hits the ball any better than you do?"

"Well if *God* can't play this game, how in blazes are *we* supposed to!"

I smiled, feeling good about the question.

"Oh, He can play all right. He's just not very good."

I moved in for the kill. "So you want me to believe that God created a game that even God in all His power and glory and perfection can't play to perfection?"

"Hey... Give Him a break. You're lucky He created it at all. It wasn't easy. He had to lay it on Earth before all the bugs were ironed out. Golf was definitely a rush job for God."

"A rush job..."

"You know. Like the avocado. Great food, but look at the size of the seed! What can I tell you... Also a rush job."

"Okay, okay... then I just have one more question and then we're finished. You're telling me golf was a rush job? So... Who rushes God?"

The Pro Upstairs smiled and did that thing with his eyebrows again. Only this time it wasn't Magnum P.I. he reminded me of.

It was the Devil.

The Devil You Say!

"So you want to know how God could create a game that even He can't play? He had no choice. Either He did something fast or the Prince of Darkness — old Satan himself — was going to beat Him to the punch. You see, in the beginning, golf belonged to the Devil. It was all his idea."

Somehow that didn't surprise me. "You know, that's the first thing you've said that makes sense," I told him.

"The Devil had been working on the game for some time. It was beautiful. Nothing could touch it for leading you Earthlings down the path to humiliation, despair, larceny —"

"Yeah. All the good stuff that keeps us coming back for one more round," I felt compelled to add.

"Exactly! But that wasn't enough for old Lucifer. He wanted to make it even more sadistic, more diabolical. So he started to mess around with greens on floating islands that pitched and rolled like the deck of a ship as soon as you hit your putt. And he put hot coals on each tee."

"Hot coals!"

"Not a bad idea, actually. Helped speed up play. It took a week just to play nine holes! The game was a bitch. You see the Devil figured it was his one chance to leave his mark on Earth. A few square miles of hell here, a couple of hundred acres of purgatory there..."

"How do you know so much about all this? I thought you were The Pro *Up*stairs?"

"I am. But I was The Pro *Down*stairs first. That's the American way, isn't it? Start at the bottom and work your way to the top!" He was smiling broadly now, and bounced his eyebrows in delight, setting off a mini-burst of sparkles from the gold Pro Upstairs logo on his visor.

I let the fireworks subside before forging ahead. I had to admit the little guy was getting to me. As outrageous as what he was telling me was, it was also kind of logical — in a nightmarish sort of way. I had to know more.

"So you were the Devil's golf pro, right?"

"You got it, Sport. You're looking at the original scratch player!"

"You shot par on a course with moving greens and hot coals?"

"What can I tell you? It was hell! The game was so tough you had to cheat. The Devil wanted to make it the hardest game to play, but the easiest to cheat at. What could be more tempting to you Earthlings?"

"He was right about that," I admitted.

"That's the part Satan was working on when I started to get worried. Cheating was all part of the game — it was legal — until you were caught..."

"And then what?"

"If you were caught, you had to sell your soul to the Devil if you still wanted to par the hole. But even that wasn't enough for Satan. That's when he came up with the bright idea of putting quicksand in the bunkers."

"Quicksand?!"

"In the beginning golf belonged to the Devil... The game was hell!"

"I mean, the game already had all the heartbreaking, ego shattering stuff you could ask for. Fun is fun... But enough's enough! That's when I took a hike upstairs. Told God that if He didn't create golf first, there'd be everlasting hell to pay on Earth."

"What did He say?"

"Well, He was kind of busy at the time. Said it was just a game. Didn't see the harm in it. But I was ready for that. So I suggested He play a few holes with me and see for Himself." The Pro paused and looked up as if replaying the scene in his mind. A small smile of peace and contentment played on his face.

"And?"

"Oh... He was Godawful. He immediately saw how damnable golf was and agreed to work on it. You know, clean it up. Of course He asked me to teach Him. He was going to master golf, perfect it — as only He could — and then He'd send it to Earth with a new name on it. Golf."

"You mean it wasn't called golf before?"

"Of course not. What kind of a name is golf? When the devil had it, he called it Flog. Now that describes the game! So God just turned it around and flog became golf."

"The way most of us play it, it might as well be flog," I said.

"I know. And I warned Him. I told God, I know you're a perfectionist. I know how you like to work, but golf's a real bitch. Even with me as your Pro, you're not going to have time to perfect it if you're going to beat the Devil at his own game. I told Him to make a few quick changes and go for it. He'd have time to master it upstairs and then send revisions down as necessary."

I was ready to say something, thought better of it, and just looked at this strange little person in front of me. Of course his story was crazy. But what did I expect from someone who called himself The Pro Upstairs?

' You can't even live by ten simple Commandments. God knows what you'll do with Nine Commandments just for golf! '

I smiled benevolently and said, "You don't really expect me to believe any of that, do you?"

"Let me put it this way, Sport. You have a better explanation of why Earthlings act the way they do when they get on a golf course? Not to mention what they go through when they can't play!"

I didn't. In fact, the more I thought about the Pro's story with the Devil, the more what I had seen and done on a golf course for 30 years made sense!

"All right. All right. I'll admit the game does seem to have its roots closer to hell than heaven," I finally answered.

"And you guys haven't done a whole lot to make it any better!" The Pro shot back. "That's why I'm here."

"I was wondering when you were going to get to the bottom line."

"Well, here it is, Sport. So listen good. In the past, a lot of God's ideas for Earth haven't worked out exactly as He would've liked."

"That's for sure..." I muttered.

The Pro let it pass. "Take that Moses thing. You know, the 86 Commandments?"

"You mean The Ten Commandments, don't you?"

"Actually it was supposed to be 86, but you guys haven't even gotten the first ten right yet! God's got 76 more for you. When you're ready. That's my point. You can't even live by ten simple Commandments. God knows what you'll do with Nine Commandments just for golf! Actually, even *He* doesn't know. But He's got to try something!"

"I guess the game is getting a little out of hand," I said. "Clubs that will do everything but hit the ball for you. Two-foot putts for a million dollars..."

"It's Sodom and Gomorrah all over again!" said the Pro.

"You know what they say, Pro. What goes around, comes around," I chimed in.

"Exactly what I told God. You beat old Lucifer to the punch in

23

> ' Then there was
> Trevino. Was a real
> favorite of God's... Was
> all set to send me down
> with the Commandments
> and turn Trevino into a
> Mexican Moses! '

the beginning. He's been working hard ever since to turn golf back to what He had in mind to begin with. I told the Lord straight out, you better find the man for me to deliver these Nine Commandments to before the game's completely shot to hell! That's when we ran into a little problem."

"Why? Just give the Commandments to one of the superstars," I said. Seemed rather obvious to me.

"God had the same idea. Been working on it for some time. Was all set to give the Commandments to someone people would listen to. Had his eye on Walter Hagan for a while there. Walt was beginning to come around. Began saying things like, 'You're only here for a short visit. Don't hurry, don't worry...' "

" 'And be sure to smell the flowers along the way,' " I finished. "Hagan was great. He would've been perfect."

"Nope. Too flashy for God. Then there was Trevino. Was a real favorite of God's. But He couldn't get Lee's attention, so He zapped him with lightning and Lee started saying things like, 'When God wants to play through, you let Him play through!' God loved that line. Was all set to send me down with the Commandments and turn Trevino into a Mexican Moses!"

"Sounds good to me."

"Too good. Which is exactly what I told God. I said, "Trevino makes shots that even *You* can't conceive! Give him the Commandments and who's gonna believe him. They'll figure Trevino can say anything he wants. Anyone who can make a hole-in-one on the 17th at PGA West against Nicklaus, Palmer and Zoellar with $175,000 on the line isn't playing the game as the rest of us!"

"You've got a point," I smiled.

"So we decided to hold a lottery! No pros allowed. Just folks who share the humiliation and frustration of golf with millions of others." The Pro looked directly at me, his eyes dancing in the twilight of this

Christmas Eve night.

"Me..." I gulped.

"You. But I gotta tell you, we almost had to throw you back."

"Why?"

"You were too calm, too even tempered. You even enjoyed the game after making a couple of double bogeys. You were almost as bad as God. Just glad to be out on the course. I was all ready to give up on you, when just now you started acting like a real golfer."

"I did?"

"Sure. Got off your high horse. Took the Lord's name in vain. Threw your driver into that tree. That was enough for me. So I threw it back and... Here we are!"

"Yeah. Here we are. So now what's supposed to happen?" I was almost afraid to ask.

"What do you say we play a few holes?"

"But it's dark. We won't be able to see anything..."

The words were hardly spoken when The Pro smiled, bounced his eyebrows and the 12th hole lit up in a shaft of light pouring out of a single star.

My mouth dropped open. I was speechless. I guess The Pro understood because he said:

"Thanks, Sport. Don't mind if I do."

The Pro stepped up on the tee and reached out his right hand to the side, palm up. It was the matter of fact gesture of a surgeon expecting his nurse to slap the correct instrument into his hand.

POOPH! In a mini-burst of stardust a wooden club appeared in The Pro's hand. He gave a quick waggle of the clubhead and set up to make a swing. Since I didn't see any ball, I assumed it was going to be a practice swing. The Pro took a smooth, full backswing. There was the slightest pause at the top when POOPH! another tiny burst of light and a golf ball sparkling like the Hope Diamond appeared, floating just off the ground as if held up by an invisible tee.

Still at the top of his beautiful full backswing, The Pro averted his eyes towards me, bounced his eyebrows, then swung through the shot in what seemed like slow motion. There was no sound when he made contact, but the ball took off into the night like a shooting star. I watched it leave a trail of stardust as it vanished far down the dark fairway. It was the most beautiful thing I'd ever seen. I was truly awestruck. If this was what golf was like in heaven, I was ready to ask for a starting time. And then I heard...

"Kind of like good sex."

"Huh?" I was still mesmerized by the tee shot.

"Good golf is like good sex," The Pro said.

"Sure. Right... Uh.. Don't tell me that is one of the Nine Commandments?"

The Pro gave a wicked little smile. I had the distinct feeling this was going to be a playing lesson I'd never forget.

PART II

The 9 Commandments
of Golf

The First Commandment

The Pro Upstairs stepped off the tee. Nervously, I took my driver, moved to the tee, and took a practice swing. It felt pretty good.

"Lovely," said The Pro. "Chester Babcock couldn't have done it any better."

"Chester Babcock? Never heard of him."

"That's right, Sport. Had the most beautiful golf swing there was — until you put a ball in front of him."

"Thanks a lot, Pro."

"Actually, I prefer Prope. That's what my friends call me."

"Prope?"

"Short for The Pro Upstairs. Just like Pope with an 'r'. Has a nice ring to it, don't you think?" He smiled, pleased with himself.

So now I was supposed to put my best swing on this ball in front of the Prope himself.

"Might as well get it over with," I said to myself. I swung and hit a hard, ugly duck hook. The exact same shot that got me into this mess in the first place!

"Ugh huh..." mused The Pro in deep thought.

"I know. Chester Babcock," I said before he could.

He looked seriously at me. "You said something just before you swung. What was it?"

"I don't know... Might as well get it over with. Something like that," I answered.

"Might as well get it over with... Is that what you say to yourself just before sex?"

"Of course not. Don't be ridiculous. Why would I want to get it over with? Sex is great."

"I bet you like it so much you wish it would last longer than it does."

"Sounds good to me," I smiled.

"Then why don't you do it in golf? All I ever hear down here is 'Miss it quick' and 'Get it over with'. Ever thought of experiencing and enjoying the golfing act as much as the sex act? You know there's not a whole lot of difference between 'em."

"Funny, that's what my wife, Barbara, said. She figured out that golf and sex were just alike. She said you didn't have to be good at either one to enjoy them."

"True! But you ever notice how the more you enjoy it, the better you become at it. You Earthlings talk all the time about spending the whole weekend in bed with your lovers."

"Well, most of us spend more time talking about it than doing it," I had to admit.

"Just like golf! You think about it and talk about it more than you do it. That's my point. There's not much to choose between them. Golf is lovemaking. At once the most glorious and obscene four letter act you Earthlings engage in."

"Well, I don't know I agree with that."

"Did I ask for your opinion? Listen to me. I'm talking about golf and sex here! The field of play looks so inviting and tempting from afar. Like a seductive smile from an attractive person. You know nothing can possibly come of it, but you can't help but smile back and wiggle your feet. It's amazing how you Earthlings are always attracted to something with the scent of danger, of mystery. Something with the promise of heart thumping ecstasy and near certainty of heartbreaking failure and frustration. Of course, when it is good and right, it is pure and sweet..."

He smiled the smile of angels. It didn't last long.

"On the other hand, when golf and sex are bad, it feels awkward, ugly, shameful! X-rated in the mind and on your scorecard. Which is probably why the very idea of spending a whole weekend in the middle of your backswing is terrifying to you. And yet isn't that what you play golf for? To experience your golf swing? So why don't you let yourself enjoy it? Feel how it feels to swing that club. Experience those precious seconds to the fullest. It's over with quick enough. Just like sex. Well, at least for some of you."

The little guy had a point — at least as far as my golfing was concerned. It got me to thinking. "You know, it's almost like your first sexual experience..."

"Speak for yourself, Sport."

"You know what I mean. You're worried. Afraid. Nervous. Not able to enjoy it as much as you thought."

"That's because in golf no matter how long you play, every shot is the *first time* all over again. And the first time means the unknown. Scary thought, isn't it?"

The Pro was enjoying watching me squirm. "It's the nature of the game. A never-ending series of first ever challenges. Almost like the real world!"

"What do you mean, almost?"

"Well, in the real world — but I'm getting ahead of myself. You're not ready for the big commandments yet. I'm not so sure you understand the first one."

"Maybe that's because I haven't heard it. All you've been talking about is sex."

*"Good golf is like good sex. The more you can feel that moment divine...
the better it is!"*

"That's about all there really is to the First Commandment. Good golf starts with being aware of what your body feels like when you do it. Don't bother your mind about whether you are doing it right. You don't think about right or wrong when you and your wife are — then again, maybe *you* do!"

"No I don't! But I understand what you're getting at. I should just try to feel what's going on."

"Don't be afraid to be completely involved in the moment. Slow down. Allow yourself to feel what's happening when you swing. It's the only way your body can relate to the golf shot it produces. And then you can make natural adjustments to change the results. Hell, it happens too fast for your mind to be any help. Now, you think you've got it?"

"Sure."

"Okay. So what's the First Commandment?"

"Think of sex...when you take your golf swing."

"No. Don't think! *Feeeeel.* The First Commandment of Golf is simply: Good golf is like good sex. The more you can feel that moment divine... the better it is!"

I thought about it for a moment, then had to smile. "You know, I'm not sure exactly what that's going to do for my golf swing, but I think my wife's going to love it!"

The little guy grinned. "Just call me the Dr. Ruth of foreplay. Now, let's go find your ball."

"Are you kidding? It's gone. We'll never find it." I wanted to forget that shot and start over, but my friend had other ideas.

"I'll find it. Trust me... Have I lied to you, yet?"

The Second Commandment

We left the tee and started to walk down the fairway, which was softly lit from the light of that single star.

"It's pretty dark over there with all those trees. Why don't I just drop a ball over here and —"

"Need a bit more light, do you, Sport?"

The Pro looked up and bounced his eyebrows. I watched as the moon began to burn through a small fogbank. It looked as though someone was turning up a dimmer switch as the moonlight melted the fog away. The 12th hole was now bathed in an incredibly warm glow from the moon and the star above it.

The Pro smiled, "I didn't hear your ball hit the trees so you probably caught the rough or went through to the other fairway here."

"Probably..." I found it hard to concentrate on looking for my ball. "I'll just drop another and..."

"Don't have to. Here it is," The Pro said, pointing over towards some trees.

As I approached, I could see the ball was sitting down in some thick grass. The best I could hope for would be to hack it back into the fairway. Unless my new teacher had something better in mind.

"Don't look at me, Sport!" He must have known what I was

thinking and said, "You got yourself into this, get yourself out."

"Isn't there another Commandment for situations like this?" It couldn't hurt to try.

"For a lie like that?" He smiled and shook his head.

"Well, it's not *that* bad."

"Then stop complaining and hit the sucker!"

I pulled out my pitching wedge, choked up, aimed back across towards the middle of the fairway and was all ready to take my swing. Then I stopped. This was my first test, I knew It. I looked up to the Pro and smiled, as much to myself as him.

"Good sex," I whispered to myself. "The more I can feel what's going on, the better it is!"

I relaxed, took a deep breath and put a smooth, solid, swing through the ball. To my surprise it shot out of the rough and flew high across the fairway into a thick stand of trees on the other side.

"Damn!"

"Too much sex can also get you into trouble," The Pro quipped.

When we got to the trees on the other side of the fairway, The Pro seemed to have lost interest in helping me find my ball. He just stood there looking up waiting for me to get on with it.

I have to admit I got a little irritated and finally blurted out, "Well, if that's all the help you're going to be, I'll just drop another ball..."

His eyes came down and settled on me with a meaningful look. "You know, Sport, I'm a different kind of pro than you have here on Earth."

"I've noticed."

"I'm more what you'd call an allopathic pro."

"Allopathic?" I had never heard the term before, though it sounded like I should have.

"Means to explore all paths..."

His eyes slowly rolled back up and I couldn't help but follow his

' I pulled my faithful old MT 3-wood out, tried to feel sexy, took a full slow backswing and drove my hips through the shot with passion. '

gaze until I saw a golf ball cradled between a couple of branches about four feet over his head.

"Holy..."

"There are many paths from the first tee to the 18th green..." he said meaningfully.

"You don't expect me to —"

"The road less traveled may be the most exciting journey of all!"

"Yeah. Right..." I mumbled and grabbed the longest iron out of my bag.

"Now we'll see what kind of a player you really are, Sport."

I proceeded to take a couple of overhead practice swings just to get the feel. I knew I'd have little chance to make solid contact with my ball, but if I could shake up the branches clutching it, I might be able to knock it back into play.

I took another overhead practice swing when I heard:

"Hit it already! It's an easy shot. Now if it had landed in some little birdie's nest... Then you'd have something to worry about!"

Without further ado I reared back and took an all out overhead swipe at the branches holding my ball captive.

The impact sent shock waves through my entire body. The branches were less forgiving than they looked. I immediately let go of my club and covered my head as twigs and other tree parts rained down around me.

"Did you see my ball?" I asked The Pro. The words were barely spoken when my golf ball plopped to the ground a few feet away, hit an exposed tree root and caromed out into the fairway.

"Well done!" said The Pro.

"I was a lumberjack in my previous life," I grinned.

We walked the few yards to where my ball now rested in the fairway. I was there in three while some 35 yards ahead The Pro's ball was in perfect position in one.

I must have had quite a hang-dog expression on my face as I studied my fourth shot because The Pro said...

"What's the matter now? Thinking about the numbers? Three gone and thinking about making six or seven... or worse!"

"You know what they say. It's not how, it's **how many**. The scorecard only has space for the numbers."

"Then maybe it's time to forget the numbers and the scorecard."

He was probably right, but I wasn't about to say so. I looked ahead to the 12th green in the distance. I had played the hole enough times to know that it was all I could hit to reach the green. It was probably 215 yards to clear the trap in front and then who knew how many yards back to the pin which looked to be fairly deep.

"Knock it stiff," said The Pro.

I pulled my faithful old MT 3-wood out, tried to feel sexy, took a full slow backswing and drove my hips through the shot with passion. It felt easy and natural. And wonderful!

The ball flew high and long and straight for the green. It was too far away for me to see it land, but I didn't need to. I knew I couldn't have hit it any better. Wherever it was, I felt sure I wouldn't need help to find it this time.

We got to The Pro's ball, and I probably don't have to tell you he hit it perfectly, with the ease of Bobby Jones, Sam Snead and Julius Boros rolled into one. His swing was a marvel of relaxed simplicity. The most natural thing in the world. But I guess that's the way it should be for The Pro Upstairs.

When we got to the green, The Pro's ball was shining brightly about 12 feet to the left of the hole. My ball was dead in line about 25 feet past.

The Pro pulled the pin as I studied the putt from both sides. I had played this hole often enough to know what I had to do. I felt absolutely confident as I hit the putt and watched it roll into the heart of the hole.

Before I could take it out, The Pro stepped up and putted. His ball hit a couple of spike holes and divot marks along the way but still managed to slide in the side door for his eagle three.

"Great three!" I said.

"Thank you. But sometimes the number is less important than what you went through to get it."

"I'll tell you one thing," I said. "I've birdied this hole a few times, but this par was even better."

"How can a par be better than a bird? After all, it's not how, it's *how many*."

"Sure. But in this case it could have been a lot more!"

"It can always be a lot more. Or less..."

"But that's true on every hole. So?" I wasn't sure what he was getting at.

"As usual, you Earthlings always get it ass backwards. It's *not* how many. It's *how*! That's the secret. You just proved it!"

"I did?"

"It's *how* you *react* to what happens to you. That's what the game is all about, Sport. It doesn't matter what happens to us, or what we get ourselves into — which is usually the case. The only thing that matters is our *reaction* to what happens. Opportunity lurks everywhere! In the sand, the rough..."

"The trees!"

"Right. You see, Sport, it's usually the dumb blunders we get ourselves into that have a way of turning into our most memorable and greatest Do Dahs!"

"Do Dahs?"

"You know, when it looks like you're really in the horse pucky, but you keep on shovelin, and somehow you ride out on the back of a beautiful buckskin pony, Do Dah, Do Dah!... But it's your choice."

"It's not how many. It's HOW!"

"That's the tough part."

"Sure it's tough! It's risky. But the riskier it is... the *more opportunity* for achieving the big Do Dah! The stuff you didn't think you had in you. Your greatest potential underneath the polyester pants!!"

Even though I was wearing jeans, I couldn't help but smile. I knew what he meant.

"You see, Sport, you have to measure opportunity with the same yardstick you measure the risk. The greater the risk, the more exciting the opportunity! That's why it's not how many. It's *how*."

"Let me take a wild guess. The Second Commandment?" I asked.

"Do I know how to slip it in there or what?" He grinned and bounced his eyebrows.

I tried bouncing mine back. Judging from The Pro's expression, I still had a lot to learn.

'Did this strange and funny little person walking beside me exist only in my head, or was he real? Was I having what they called an 'out of body experience'? Or was I just out of my mind??'

The Third Commandment

As we walked to the 13th tee, it occurred to me how lucky I was to have been picked to receive these Commandments. The moment the thought struck, it also made me laugh.

I didn't really believe all this was actually happening, did I? I had heard somewhere that we all create our own reality. Still... Did this strange and funny little person walking beside me exist only in my head, or was he real? Was I having what they called an 'out of body experience'? Or was I just out of my mind??

I was seriously considering the latter when The Pro said: "You ever notice, Sport, how wherever you go — there you are!"

"What?" I was sure I had missed something in between there.

"You feel pretty good about yourself right now, don't you? I mean, that five on the last hole sort of lifted your spirits."

I sensed The Pro was steering me toward another Commandment.

"Well, I certainly feel a lot better than I did before I made it," I admitted.

"That's because you feel good about yourself when you feel in control. Which is also the greatest problem you Earthlings have with golf."

"Why is it a problem?" I figured it was easier to feed him a straight line than to argue the point.

"Because in golf, most of the time, you have very little control. So you generally feel rotten about yourselves."

"Not me. I feel great!"

"Good. I mean you're happy and smiling now after what you did on the last hole. I just hope you can be the same way after this next hole."

Now he had me worried.

"Why? Is something terrible going to happen? What am I going to do?"

"Don't ask me. I'm not God. I'm just His Pro. But whatever you do, just remember..." the Pro paused, then very slowly said, "You are not what you do."

It was so pregnant with meaning I had to repeat it, just to make sure that was all there was.

"You are not what you do?"

"Exactly!" The Pro shot back, his eyes growing wide. "Because, if you *are* what you do, then when you *don't*... you *aren't*!"

Oh boy, now he was getting weird.

"Aren't *what*?" I said.

The Pro made a face and shrugged.

"Wait a second. You can't just say something like that and let it hang there!"

"Sure I can. I'm The Pro Upstairs," he said smugly.

"And that's one of the Commandments??" I shouted.

"Don't be ridiculous. Of course not. It was just something that came to me. Thought I'd run it up the flagstick and see what you thought. Let's see now... Guess I'm up!"

He jumped up on the 13th tee and proceeded to smooth a drive just short of the green on this 314 yard par four hole.

"God, I love this game!" he babbled. "Your turn, Sport. Looks

'You only forget what you don't experience for yourself. Believe me, by the time I'm through with you, you'll remember.'

like an easy straight shot. I'm sure you've got nothing to worry about. Except for the trees on the right. And the Carmel River on the left."

My hand moved from my driver to my 3-wood. To my surprise I hit it solid down the left center of the fairway.

When I got to my ball, I could see The Pro's ball ahead just short of the green.

I pulled out my wedge, tried to experience the feeling of the shot and knocked it about eight feet to the right of the hole. That First Commandment was really working! I really felt every second of that swing.

For the first time I began not to care if this was real or just a dream. What worried me was that if it was a dream, I wouldn't remember the Commandments when I woke up. Then I remembered a little note pad I used to keep in my bag. I had put it there a year earlier when I was working on another book. I started looking through my bag for it when...

"Now what are you doing?" The Pro asked somewhat irritably.

"Trying to find a note pad. I wanted to write down some of this stuff..."

"STUFF?!" yelped The Pro like a wounded puppy. "The Nine Commandments are life itself. Stuff is everything else!"

"I'm sorry. I just didn't want to forget it."

"You only forget what you don't experience for yourself. Believe me, by the time I'm through with you, you'll remember."

There was nothing more to say on the matter, as far as The Pro Upstairs was concerned, and he turned and strode toward his ball.

The little guy stroked his approach to within a foot of the cup, walked onto the green, then casually backhanded it in for an easy birdie three.

I looked over my eight footer from both sides and put a good roll on it. The ball hit the left lip and spun out.

45

"Mmmmmm," said The Pro. "Thought you had it."

"So did I," I answered as I walked to the hole and casually back-handed my ten incher for par. Except it didn't go in. The ball spun out of the hole and ended up over a foot away.

I swallowed hard. "Well... It was a gimme, anyway," I whimpered.

"Then you should have made it. Now you've got an even longer one."

I took a deep breath, stepped up and rolled it in the hole for the bogey five. I grabbed my ball out of the hole, angry with myself for missing the one before.

I fully expected to hear some words of wisdom from The Pro, but he just looked at me with a sad smile of disappointment and shook his head.

The look was worse than anything he could have said. At least I could respond to verbal abuse, but those eyes and that look made me feel like an unworthy jackass.

"Well, say *something*! I'm a screw-up. Come on. I know you've got something to say about it. Let me have it."

The Pro said nothing. Then turned and started to walk away.

"Wait a minute! Where are you going? You can't just walk away!... I mean, isn't there a Commandment for something like this?"

The Pro stopped and turned back to me. "Sure there's a Commandment, Sport. And you already know it."

"I do?..." Then it hit me. "Ahhh! It's not how many. It's *how*!"

"Were we playing the same hole?" The Pro said sarcastically. "The way it looked to me, the *how* was pathetic."

"All right. I missed a little tap-in. But I didn't really try," I babbled. "I could've made it if I'd tried."

"I know. I saw. You thought you *had it* before you took the trouble to *get it*. You know, Sport, the Devil was no fool. He knew that if golf could easily swell your Earthly egos, it could just as easily

"The minute you think you've got golf... it's got you."

put an ice pick through 'em. To the Devil it was absolute Heaven. Which, of course, makes it Hell for you. But it doesn't have to be. Not with the Third Commandment."

"All right. I'm hooked. What is it?"

"The minute you think *you've* got golf... it's got *you*."

"I knew that."

"Of course you knew it! Anybody who's ever played the game knows it. But I guess you Earthlings would just as soon ignore it so you can bitch, bitch, bitch, bitch, bitch, bitch, bitch, bitch..."

And he was off to the next tee.

The Third Commandment

The minute you think you've got golf... it's got you.

D. GOODWIN

"*Keep your nose out of the other guy's putts!*"

Keep Your Nose Out Of The Other Guy's Putts

As we walked to the 14th tee on the other side of the Carmel River, I couldn't help but think about the tap-in putt I had missed and the same kind of putt The Pro had made.

"I've got a question. What do you say when somebody says golf really isn't... you know... fair?"

"Are you still carping over that little putt I made and the one you didn't?"

"No. I just wanted —"

"Yes you are. You Earthlings have always had a real hard time keeping your nose out of each others' putts. Probably should have made that a Commandment. Keep your nose out of the other guy's putts! What I do — or anyone else does — has nothing to do with what you do. You don't play golf against anyone but yourself. It's just you, the ball, and all that dumb stuff you do to yourself. You know that."

"Yes, I know that. But —"

"No buts. You want to play better golf, then stop focusing on what the other guy is doing. You think Paul Runyon would have had a chance to beat Sam Snead in the 1938 P.G.A. if he'd really thought about what Sam was doing to him off the tee? Hell, Sam was outdriving Runyon 40, 50, 60 yards on every hole. We're talking David and Goliath here! Runyon was hitting 3-woods to the green compared to Snead's 8- and 9-irons. Didn't concern Runyon. Since he was so short he was always first to hit, knocked it dead on the pin and put the pressure on Snead. Made Sam more concerned with what Runyon was going to do than keeping his mind on his own game. Beat Snead eight and seven. Slammed the door on the slammer."

"You know, Pro, I think you made a mistake. Keep your nose out of the other guy's putts should be a Commandment."

"Hey, just because it's not one of mine... If the nose fits..." The Pro bounced his eyebrows, turned and stepped up on the 14th tee.

"What have we got?" The Pro said.

"See those trees up ahead. Stay just to the left of them, then it's a short iron dead left back across the river to the green. It's really a lay up the way you hit the ball."

"And the way you hit the ball?" he asked looking me square in the eyes.

"It's all I can hit with my nose," I smiled.

The Fourth Commandment

The Pro Upstairs stepped to the tee, held out his palm and POOPH! a 2-iron was in his hand. And then that easy, smooth swing and the ball took off, its comets tail of sparkles making a perfect right to left path as the ball headed straight for the trees, then curved gently to the left and bounded into the narrowing neck at the end of the fairway.

Again I went for my 3-wood, took aim and put what felt like a good swing on it. I never did see the ball.

"Felt good," I said to The Pro. "But I never saw it."

"Shouldn't matter. What did you see before you hit it?"

"Before I hit it? How could I see anything before I hit it?" I should have known it was a set-up. The Pro bounced his eyebrows and I knew what was coming.

"Why is it I feel a Commandment coming on?" I cracked.

"Either you have incredible psychic powers... Or you're finally getting the hang of this gig. Or —"

"Nevermind! Just tell me the Commandment."

"Actually the way the Fourth Commandment originally went wasn't nearly as good as the way Einstein said it."

"You mean Albert Einstein?"

"No, Skippy Einstein. Of course, Albert Einstein!"

"I've never heard about him playing golf," I told The Pro.

"Of course not. Ahhhh... but he would have been one of the greats! Al knew that your imagination is your preview of golf's coming attractions!"

"Obviously the words of a low handicapper," I said facetiously.

The Pro let it pass. "What he really said was 'Your imagination is your preview of *life's* coming attractions.' I changed it to golf's coming attractions. But I don't think Al would mind. The man knew what it was all about. So did a bunch of the big hitters. And they weren't even golfers! Take that Thoreau. You know, the fella who wrote about some other guy's lake..."

"I think you mean Walden Pond."

"Whatever. Anyway, he said 'If you advance confidently in the direction of your dreams and endeavor to live the life you have *imagined*, you will meet with a success unexpected in common hours.' Had to be talking about golf!"

"Well, I suppose you —"

"And what about: 'It is a poor sort of memory that only remembers the past. Imaginative thinking remembers the future!' You know who said that?"

"Mmmmmm. Nope. I give up."

"Oh... I was hoping you would, since I forgot... Lewis Carroll! That's the one. The guy who wrote *Alice In Wonderland*."

"Figures. 'Imaginative thinking remembers the future...' " I had my doubts about that one. But the Pro was on a roll now.

"You see, the only way you can remember the future is to imagine it *first*! Whatever you can hold in your mind — visualize in great detail — you can achieve, you can be! Now, if you had imagined how you wanted your shot to go, and seen exactly where it was going to go *before* you hit, then when you hit it and it felt good, you wouldn't need to see where it went. Or ask me. You'd knooooow."

"Your imagination is your preview of golf's coming attractions!"

"Ok. But I didn't imagine the shot first. And I didn't see it after I hit it. And you didn't either. So now what?"

"So now you're up shit creek."

"Says you. I'll find it."

"Sure you will. When you do just try and remember the Fourth Commandment."

"Your imagination is your preview of golf's coming attractions?"

"You got it, Sport."

I breathed a small sigh of relief.

"Actually, now that I think about it, the Fourth Commandment may not be enough. Not with the shot you've got coming up."

The Pro gave me a smile that must of been a holdover from his days with the Prince of Darkness. Then he turned, did a little Scottish jig, and was off down the fairway.

The Fifth Commandment

I caught up with The Pro 50 yards down the 14th fairway.

"Have you ever noticed, Sport, that those Earthlings who really seem to enjoy golf the most and play it the best, have a certain creative spark? Actors, musicians... even politicians love the game. Your lawyers are notorious golf fanciers. It's not surprising they can be just as creative defending a client as they can be in finding a good lie in the rough."

"What was that?" I admit my mind was still contemplating what lay ahead.

The Pro stopped walking. "You think I'm out here to hear myself talk! Is that what you think, Sport?"

"No. Of course not —"

"Good. Because I don't need these Commandments! I've got other things to do. In fact, if you wanna know the truth, I've got a starting time in less than an hour with Jones and Cruikshank and Crosby."

"You mean Bobby, Bobby, and Bing??"

"No. Patti, Maxine and LaVerne!... Look, Sport, if you're not up to it, just say the word and I'm out of here."

"No. Don't leave. I'm sorry. I was just thinking about —"

"I know what you were thinking about. Worrying about the shot ahead before you even know what it is. That's almost as bad as thinking about the hole you just screwed up. Don't waste your time watering yesterday's divots. Crying over the last hole's or last round's missed gimmies, banana balls, chili dips and shanks doesn't do a whole lot of good — unless you'd kinda like to hit it that way again. Which is exactly what the Devil was hoping for when he put the game together in the first place! The only reason he put divots in the game at all was so the next time you played around, the scarred ground would remind you of the hell you went through the last time."

"Which has nothing to do with this time around."

"Exactly. Which is why it takes some creative juice if you really want to master the game!"

"But what about all those non-creative people who are just as crazy about the game? What happens to them?"

"That's the incredible thing. Golf percolates deep into the heart and soul and finds that creative spark in everyone! Then it grabs hold and drags it out of you. In fact, Earthlings who spend all week working in structured and controlled jobs with no room for creative thinking are even more susceptible to becoming golf addicts."

"Makes sense," I said. "When they get to the golf course, all that creative energy buried throughout the week can burst out!"

"That's it. In golf you can let that creative genius inside run wild and naked down the fairway! And you don't even have to be good for that spark to work its magic. In fact, the more strokes you take, the more opportunities for your inspired, creative self to come up with that one miraculous shot to save the day!"

"The way you're talking reminds me of Walter Mitty." The minute I said it, I had to smile.

"You may have something there, Sport. In fact, golf may be the ultimate Walter Mitty sport. Fantasy fulfillment for all who dare to tee it up and go for it! After all, how many of you will ever get to

'How more human and mortal your golfing heroes become when the game occasionally treats them no better than it regularly treats you!'

play football in the Rose Bowl? Or shoot hoops in Madison Square Garden? Or pitch in Yankee Stadium?"

"Yeah. And if we got the chance and tried to make one of those circus catches in the end zone on a pass from Joe Montana, we'd probably break our necks."

"But you can do it all in golf! You can walk the same fairways as your golfing heroes. Dress the same. Attempt the same shots. Maybe even make one or two as good as, or even better, than your favorite pro."

"I hate to say this, but sometimes it does make you feel kinda good when the pros miss the same easy shots we miss. Probably not fair, but it does make —"

"Not fair!? NOT FAIR!?" The Pro roared. "*Life* may not be fair. I'll go with that. But *golf*? Golf is the fairest of the fair! Because it treats everybody the same."

"Well, I don't know —"

"What could be more fair than the pain and suffering golf heaps upon your backswing, it likewise doles out to the greatest players in the game? How more human and mortal your golfing heroes become when the game occasionally treats them no better than it regularly treats you! Just as you have the opportunity to live out your fantasies and be Nicklaus or Palmer — if only for a shot or two — Jack and Arnie have the same opportunity to live out their greatest nightmares and hit a couple like you! Oh, by the way — there's your ball."

The Pro gestured behind me, but before I could turn and see for myself, he said:

"Before you take a look, I think you better hear the Fifth Commandment."

"Oh shit..." I said under my breath.

"No. But how's this: Golf treats everyone the same. Except for those who don't believe it — who usually get what they deserve."

"Thanks. Can I look now?"

The Pro nodded, beaming like the Cheshire Cat in *Alice In Wonderland*.

The Fifth Commandment

Golf treats everyone the same. Except for those who don't believe it — who usually get what they deserve.

"Golf treats everyone the same. Except for those who don't believe it —
who usually get what they deserve."

The Voice Of Daring!

I looked down and found my ball sitting in a little hollow with hard pan and roots under it. It was not a pretty sight.

"Now look up?" The Pro said.

I did, and found myself staring at the girth of an enormous cottonwood tree six feet in front of me and squarely between my ball and the 14th green, which was approximately 130 yards away across the river. A couple of feet one side or the other and I would have had a shot. But this?

"So... Golf treats everyone the same. Except for those who don't believe it — who usually get what they deserve?" I said sarcastically. "You planned it this way, didn't you?"

"Well, I may have had a little to do with it, but... there are no accidents! *You* planned it this way as much as I. How else could you experience the truth of these Commandments? What would you learn and remember if you didn't have to play them out for yourself? You Earthlings always say, 'Learn from the mistakes of others.' Horse feathers! The only way to learn anything is to make all the mistakes *yourself*!"

The Pro walked away towards his ball up ahead. It was in perfect position with no more than a wedge to the green. Halfway there he stopped and turned back.

"Remember, Sport... Imagination is the voice of daring!"

Okay, if that's the way he wants to play, I said to myself, I can be just as daring as... The Golden Bear! So if I was Nicklaus, I'd probably hit it high to the left and cut it back to the right over the river and over the tall tree guarding the left approach to the green.

Now if I was Gary Player, I'd probably go for a hook around the right side trying to keep it low under these branches, but up enough to still carry the river and the trap protecting the right front of the green.

I looked at my lie again. No way could I get this ball up high the way it was sitting. No, I'd have to come up with something special. Something... Ah hah! What about a slow slide around the left side, just high enough to clear the river, but low enough to stay under the branches of that tall tree over there. Sort of a low-high-controlled-semi-shank. One of my unique specialties!

"You want creative genius, Pro? Wait till you see this masterpiece," I said, though not really loud enough for him to hear. Which was probably a good thing since there was one other possible shot. If my aim was slightly off, I could very well hit the tree directly in front of me, sending the ball screaming back for a hole-in-one in my head. And then I'd be on my way upstairs just in time to caddie for Bobby, Bobby, and Bing!

I looked up ahead to where The Pro was standing, or rather used to be. Because now I saw the Slammer himself standing there. Snead looked back to me, and in his trademark West Virginia drawl said: "You're away, son."

I wondered how Paul Runyon would've played this shot. Then I remembered The Pro's words: "Everywhere you go — there you are." While it wasn't one of his Commandments, it seemed appropriate. While I could fantasize being Nicklaus or Player or even Runyon, I'd probably have a better shot playing myself. After all, who could

"The voice of daring!"

> *' The way the ball felt coming off the face of my 6-iron was so wonderfully weird that it could only be my low-high-controlled-semi-shank. '*

do me better than me?

There was only one shot to play — against Sam Snead or The Pro Upstairs. To tell you the truth, the way The Pro was playing, I was relieved to see Snead for a change. The Pro was unbeatable but Sam Snead? What chance did he have against my specialty, the low-high-controlled-semi-shank!

The Slammer was doomed.

I pulled out my 6-iron. Took one last look at the green, then one practice swing.

I had to smile. I saw the whole thing. I swear it! No second thoughts. No more practice swings. I was going to play this shot while it was still alive in my imagination.

The way the ball felt coming off the face of my 6-iron was so wonderfully weird that it could only be my low-high-controlled-semi-shank. I didn't even try to follow the flight of my ball. I knew.

When I looked up to watch Snead's reaction, it was only The Pro again. I walked towards him while he set up to hit.

"You know that shot you just hit, Sport?"

"What happened? Go in the hole?" I asked full of myself.

"Never saw anything like it. Almost like you... shanked it."

I smiled. Then bounced my eyebrows.

The Pro laughed, so I must have been getting better.

When we got to the green, my ball was hole high. About 18 feet to the right. Just a bit too much shank on it. But I wasn't complaining. Considering where I was only minutes before, the results of my creative genius was more than... fair.

The Pro was about 13 feet from the hole on the opposite side.

I putted first. My ball stopped about six inches short. I walked up, lined it up, and knocked it in for my four.

To my surprise, The Pro missed his birdie putt and had to settle for par. We had halved the hole.

As we walked off the green, The Pro said, "Strange and wonderful, isn't it? At every turn, the opportunity for perfection — at the risk of disaster... Almost like the real world."

I slowed my pace, wanting to fully enjoy the good feeling inside before we got to the next hole. The 15th at Rancho Canada had always been my Waterloo; my Little Big Horn; my personal golfing Hell on Earth. Before reaching the tee, I stopped and turned to look back across the 14th green and the Carmel River, to where I had played my shot from behind the tree. My heart did a little dance against my chest. I felt at peace with myself and everything in the world. If I had died at that moment, I wouldn't have minded.

But alas, I was still alive and had to play the 15th hole. I turned, lifted my head and marched bravely to the gallows.

The Sixth Commandment

The 15th is a 380 yard bowling alley with trees and bushes and the Carmel River on the left, and monstrous cottonwoods on the right all the way from tee to green. Approximately 225 yards out, the landing area has a couple of trees creeping into the already narrow fairway making the area barely 20 yards wide. Just to make it even more interesting, there is an enormous tree about 60 yards short of the green on the left, so that even if you find that 20 yard landing spot on your drive, you have to draw your second around the tree on the left, unless you can lay your tee shot precisely down the right center and still keep it out of the trees.

I was all set to explain all this to The Pro, but decided to let him find out for himself. After all, according to him, it was better to keep my nose out of the other guy's putts.

Besides, after one look at the hole, he smiled and said, "Looks like the Devil himself had a hand in this one. Brings back memories. I like it!"

The Pro used his brassie, and I don't have to tell you where he hit it.

"Perfect," I muttered. Looking down the fairway, I thought of big Al's words, 'Your imagination is your preview of golf's coming attractions.' Unfortunately, all I could see was my ball taking one look

"Great expectations!"

'*You talk about the ball going to the right or the left or anywhere else and when it does, you Earthlings can't wait to whine, 'I KNEW I was going to do that.'*'

at the trouble on the left and deciding to make a major detour deep into the trees on the right.

"Look out trees, here I come," I muttered to myself. I could see the trees were terrified and would do anything to avoid being hit by my ball.

Halfway into my backswing I heard:

"What is it with you?"

"Wha?" I said, nearly falling over at the top of my backswing.

"I thought you were different. But you're just like the rest," The Pro said.

"The rest of who?"

"Earthlings. You guys would rather be right and in trouble, than wrong and in the game."

"What are you talking about?"

"I'm talking about you! Who else is here? Did somebody else say, 'Look out trees, here I come'? Why did you say that?"

"Because... You know. Saying it gets it out in the open, clears the air so you won't do it."

"Horse pucky! In this game what you say is what you get, Sport. You said what you said because it's the easy way out."

"Easy way out? How can it be easy if I'm out in the boonies?!"

"Because when you expect the worst, you are rarely disappointed. You talk about the ball going to the right or the left or anywhere else and when it does, you Earthlings can't wait to whine, 'I *knew* I was going to do that.' Of course you knew it, dummy! Where else could it go? You told yourself that's where it was going to go."

"Well, I suppose —"

"Don't interrupt. Listen, Sport, you have got to be very careful about what you talk about and think about, because you will surely get it! And I'll tell you why. Because what you think and talk about comes from your conscious mind. What you *do* comes from your subconscious! Whether you're listening to your conscious mind or not, your subconscious is!"

"Yeah, but —"

"Don't interrupt. Your mind can only react to one thought at a time — positive or negative. And your subconscious — the doer — can't respond *positively* to a negative thought. You still with me?"

"Well, I —"

"The catch is that if you say you won't hit it over there, your subconscious skips right over the 'I won't' and latches on to 'hit it over there,' so you *do*, even though you said you weren't going to. You still with me?"

"That's exactly what happens to me on uphill putts. I always say to myself, 'Don't leave it short' and —"

"And you leave it short."

"Or over react and knock it a mile past."

"Because you are talking to yourself in the *negative*! You've got to talk in the positive. 'I'm going to *get it* to the hole.' There is only one way your subconscious can react to that."

"Got it."

"All right. So stop shooting yourself in the foot and hit it down the middle."

"I'm going to nail this ball down the pipe," I said to myself as I again addressed my ball.

"What was that? I didn't quite hear it," The Pro needled.

"I'm going to nail this sucker down the pipe!" I said a little louder.

"You're going to what?" The Pro badgered again.

"I'm going to hit this friggin' ball on the green and you are going to shut up so I can do it!" I exploded.

Before The Pro could say anything else, I took one hellacious swing and sent the ball screaming high, long, and way right with a big slice deep into the trees. I turned and looked at my teacher, my golfing guru, The Pro Upstairs who supposedly had all the answers and knew all the secrets.

The little guy just shrugged and said, "Some days chickens, some days feathers."

"What the hell is that supposed to mean!"

"There's no sure thing, Sport. In this life or the next. Trust me. But if you expect good things to happen and expect to be lucky, you'll find good fortune in every go around. You can only get from golf what you expect out of it. So if you expect the worst, you'll rarely be disappointed. Expect the best... and you may surprise yourself! And that, Sport, is the Sixth Commandment."

"Expect the worst and you'll rarely be disappointed. Expect the best and you may surprise yourself..."

"Remember it."

"Got it!"

"Good. Now forget it."

"What? You just told me to remember it."

"Now I'm telling you to forget about it."

"But why should I forget it?" He was making me crazy again.

The Pro then gave me the most meaningful eyeball-to-eyeball look, as if he was about to tell me the secret of life itself.

"Because to play your best golf... it helps to be out of your mind."

"Shouldn't be hard to remember that one," I said. "I've been out of my mind since I met you. Just one question. Do you want me to remember it, or forget it?"

"Just let it ooze into your pores and sorta percolate down to your feet. By the time you get through with your next shot, you'll understand... Everything."

"To play your best golf, it helps to be out of your mind."

The Seventh Commandment

As we crossed the bridge back over the Carmel River and headed up the right side of the 15th fairway, The Pro Upstairs began whistling Moon River.

The idea that in order to play your best golf it helped to be out of your mind intrigued me, particularly since we had spent so much time discussing the mental side of the game. In fact, the Commandments up till then had all dealt with the way we think about the game. Except, of course, for the First Commandment, which seemed to relate more to our physical side: Good golf is like good sex. The more you can feel that moment divine, the better it is.

It would be hard to forget that one.

But the more I thought about The Pro's 'out of your mind' statement, the more it seemed a complete contradiction of almost everything we had been talking about.

I wanted to discuss this, but The Pro wasn't interested and just kept whistling Moon River.

To my great surprise I found my ball in the fairway. It had apparently hit the trees and kicked back out. I was at least 20 yards behind The Pro's ball, but with a fairly straight shot to the green of about 170 yards.

As I surveyed the shot, The Pro stood a few feet away watching, still whistling Moon River. I figured he'd stop and allow me some quiet when I finally addressed the ball. So I went ahead and visualized the shot I wanted to hit, told myself I was going to hit it on the green, hoping my conscious mind would relay that positive message to my subconscious, who would then tell my physical body to shape up, allowing me to then experience and feel the moment divine in all its glory.

The Pro just kept whistling Moon River. I looked over to him with a glare to cool it. He stopped.

I addressed my shot, took a waggle, and heard...

"Hey batter, batter, batter! Wait for your pitch. Wait for your pitch..."

"WHAT ARE YOU DOING!?" I screamed.

"Just trying to help you, Sport," he said.

"Help me?? By calling 'Wait for your pitch!' This isn't the World Series!!"

"You were thinking too much. I was just trying to help you get out of your mind."

"Well maybe I don't want to get out. It's *my* mind. Mind your own mind! What happened to keep your nose out of the other guy's putts? All the way down here it's Moon River and now it's Take Me Out To The Ball Game. Look, I know there's a Commandment in here someplace, so why don't you just tell me what it is. Or allow me the courtesy of QUIET so I can play this shot."

"Well since you put it like that... How 'bout if I whistle Zip-A-Dee-Do-Dah *and* you play the shot?"

I glared an unkindly suggestion at The Pro.

"Yep. This is definitely one case where God should have left well enough alone," The Pro said. "You see, Sport, the way the Devil had it, golfers were allowed to make all kinds of noises when someone

"Plenty of peace and quiet so you can think about it — and let that little voice inside have its way with you."

was hitting. Galleries could holler and razz. Just like in baseball or basketball. But God thought the game was tough enough without that, so you got quiet instead. Of course what you really got is that little voice inside telling you all the things to look out for and not to do and what'll happen if you do. Now that's really hell!"

"Aren't you forgetting all the positive thoughts and images — all the Commandments you've been teaching me?"

"Well... I hate to be the one to tell you this, but uh... sometimes they just aren't enough. Like that last shot you hit. You were talking and thinking all the right things, but look how you hit it. Ugly! Too much to think about. Now with playing partners or spectators making noise, you'd have to spend a lot of that excess mental energy blocking out that stuff. Sometimes being out of your mind is a lot better than being your own worst enemy."

He had a point. "I guess it's sort of like football when one team calls a timeout just before the other team tries a field goal. They want to let the kicker think about it."

The Pro nodded. "Only in golf you don't have to call time out to accomplish the same torture," he smiled. "It's all one big time-out. Plenty of peace and quiet so you can think about it — and let that little voice inside have its way with you."

"Yeah. And drive ourselves crazy."

"Yes, sir. You Earthlings did old Lucifer one better on that score."

I stepped back to my ball, expecting The Pro to start whistling or cat calling. Something.

Silence.

I looked over to him. "Well?"

"Well what?"

"I'm waiting for some noise, some accompaniment."

"Oh, no. I did that just to get my point across. Actually, I prefer quiet. Makes the game more interesting. Don't you think?"

"You sure you're not moonlighting for the Devil?"

The idea must have appealed to The Pro, who broke into a mephistophelian grin.

It was absolutely quiet as I prepared to hit my shot to the green.

Except I couldn't take the club back. I was paralyzed by the silence. So I started to sing. The only thing I could think of.

"Zip-a-dee-do-dah, Zip-a-dee-"

WHACK!

It was the best Zip-a-dee 5-iron I'd ever hit. Maybe The Pro was right. To play your best golf, it does help to be out of your mind!

The Seventh Commandment

To play your best golf it helps to be out of your mind.

'The more you reach for and enjoy along the way, the more the road opens up to wonderful surprises!'

The Eighth Commandment

The Pro and I sang Zip-A-Dee-Do-Dah all the way to the green. We marched along singing louder and louder.

If anybody had seen us at that moment, they would have locked us up and thrown away the key. We were most assuredly out of our minds. The Pro Upstairs, with me right behind, marched around the entire 15th green whistling and singing. Reaching the front of the green The Pro made a military left turn and marched for the flag about half way back on the green.

I was right behind as he got to the flag, saluted, and pulled the pin.

Then suddenly The Pro stopped and said, "Did you know that during a four or five hour round of golf, even if you take 100 shots, you spend less than three minutes actually hitting the ball?"

"No, I did not know that," I answered.

"Probably doesn't seem very important, does it, Sport? But you know with the exception of those three minutes hitting the ball, there's an awful lot of time in between. It's too bad you Earthlings don't appreciate it more."

"You mean like we just did?"

"We did, didn't we? You see, the true enjoyment of the game doesn't come from just the result. It has to come from the journey, the way there. Because the way is endless. And the more you reach for and enjoy along the way, the more the road opens up to wonderful surprises! Particularly since no matter how good you play, you are always going to want to play better. So the secret is to enjoy what is."

"Which **is** a whole lot of just getting from here to there," I said.

"That's it, my friend."

It took a second for me to realize it was the first time he hadn't called me Sport.

"The Eighth Commandment is simply to learn to enjoy the time in between — there's so much of it! Because it will be the same **you** here tomorrow. So why not learn to appreciate today? Now. This second..."

We stood silent. There was something I wanted to say, but I was hesitant to break the moment.

Finally I whispered two of the least liked words in golf.

"You're away."

The Eighth Commandment

Learn to enjoy
the time in
between — there's
so much of it.

D. GOODWIN

The Ninth Commandment

The Pro was about ten feet left of the hole. I was a bit closer on the right side. The Pro took very little time to line up the putt and was all ready to stroke it when he looked up and gave me a curious little chuckle.

I smiled back, wondering what was going on in that strange little head.

The Pro hit his putt and the ball rolled straight for the hole, hit the right center of the cup and made a complete 360 degree trip around the lip before coming to rest on the edge. He had missed.

The Pro walked to the hole, took a closer look to see if the ball had any chance to fall in, then knocked it in for his par.

"It's up to you, Sport. Knock it in and you beat me."

"I know," I said gleefully. I knew my putt would break a little right towards the ocean. All I had to do was put a smooth stroke on it.

I was all set to go for it. But The Pro wasn't.

"You don't really want to sink it and beat me, do you?"

"Of course I do!"

"After all I've done for you? You'd really do that to the old Pro here?" He said it with a sorrowful whimper.

"What are you trying to do to me!"

"I think it is you, my son, who are trying to do it to me."

"Come on. It's been Sport all along. Then it was friend. And now my son? Come on. Don't do this..."

The Pro looked at me with his sad puppy face, then said, "Too much, huh?"

In a flash the real Pro Upstairs was back — along with the devilish smile which left no doubt as to his roots.

"Definitely too much. Now if you'll excuse me, I'd like to make this putt." I turned back to the job at hand.

"Can't it wait?"

"No. Just give me a second. I'm all set."

"Don't worry. You can't miss. Trust me..."

He gave me a smile, half from Heaven and half from the bowels of Hades.

"All right! What is so important it can't wait until I make this putt... and beat you?" I asked smiling.

"The Ninth Commandment. This is one of the big ones, Sport."

"Okay. What is it?"

"Actually, now that I think about it, you might get more out of it after you putt."

"Make up your mind!"

"Okay. Are you going to be happier if you make this putt than if you miss it?"

"Of course. What kind of —"

"You're right. Next question. Do par shooters have more fun than players who shoot a hundred?"

"Sure. That's the whole idea —"

"Wrong! Because whether you shoot par or 150, you Earthlings always think you'll be happier if you could trim just a couple more strokes from your score. You're always wanting more, so you're never satisfied with less. You still don't get it, do you? Happiness in golf is not something you can ever arrive at. It certainly isn't par. It is not any place you can reach. The answer to happiness on the golf course can only come from the game itself. From playing."

"Then how come I am happier when I shoot lights out?"

"Maybe it's because you *played* lights out. People who get fully involved in play usually achieve much greater results than those who try so hard. The more you try to beat golf, the less chance you have of doing it. Chasing lower golf scores is like trying to grab a handful of water. The tighter you squeeze, the less water you have! Not until you are able to transcend your score — understand the joy of simply playing — will you be able to master the game."

"But if you're really scoring miserably, it's tough to have a great time."

"Sure, anybody can be happy when they're scoring well. And it's easy to be onery when you're scoring badly. So when you're not scoring well, you have to find some other aspect of your play to get excited about. I mean let's face it, if your putting is bad, no matter what else you're doing, you're not going to score very well. But maybe you're hitting the ball good. So focus on your ball-striking and enjoy that part of your game."

"But what if you're putting lousy and you're hitting the ball lousy, and —"

"So in that case maybe losing less than half a dozen balls makes it a happy day. Or maybe just the fact that the birds are singing, the trees are in blossom, the sky is clear and you're —"

"Well what if it's cold and raining and you can't find your ball because the fairways are covered with leaves and the ducks are quacking in the middle of your backswing and the guy you're playing with is a 28 handicapper, but thinks he's ready for the tour and is telling you how to do it after every shot?"

"Things could be worse. You could be playing with your dentist —

"Golf is happiness!"

at his place — and he's not replacing his divots!"

"What was the Ninth Commandment again?" I asked before he could come up with any other ideas.

"The first priority in golf is simply to enjoy it, because... here it comes, Sport... The big one... There is no way to happiness in golf. Golf *is* happiness."

"Golf is happiness... That's it?"

"That's EVERYTHING you nincompoop! Happiness is well-being. And **being well** is what golf's all about! The game is good for what ails you. You just have to keep swinging! A round of golf is as therapeutic as anything in a doctor's bag. Hell, when Alister Mackenzie convinced all his regular patients to take up golf and they did, he never saw 'em again — except on the links. So he took his own advice, quit the doctoring and became a golf course architect. Designed Cypress Point and Augusta National for Bobby Jones, he did."

"I didn't know he was a doctor?" I offered sheepishly. From the look in his eyes, The Pro was about to operate on me.

"Why, the game of golf is the best therapy in the world 'cause it squeezes you good. And you know what comes out?"

"Uhhh..."

"What's inside! That's what comes out. All the anger and frustration and fear that clogs the arteries and the spirit and makes you old before your time. Golf's better than a four-hour enema for cleaning out your insides. Golf's the elixer of youth! You're never too old to be young on the golf course. All the things you aren't supposed to do in the rest of your life, you can do on the golf course playground. You can be a kid again. Wear funny clothes and hats. Play with your own bag of toys. And then you can laugh at your own damn foolishness. And that's the healthiest thing of all! Because laughter jiggles your guts. Tickles your insides. Laughter is the catalyst for great expectations!"

"I'm sorry. You're right. Golf is all of those things..."

"And they all add up to joy and well being and..."

"And the score shouldn't matter, I know... But then why do I still want to make this putt so badly? It matters. I can't help it."

"Well... You're only human. No offense." He looked gravely at me. "Do what you have to."

At least I had to give it a try. I took another look at the putt from behind, set myself over the ball, took a deep breath and —

"I can't let you go through with it, Sport."

I didn't move. It was too late to stop now.

"Try and stop me," I muttered as I took my putter back. .

"Have it your way," I heard him say.

I never looked up as I brought my putter squarely into the back of the ball...

The Ninth Commandment

Golf
is
happiness!

D. GOODWIN

'You will see that these secrets for mastering the game are spread among the people so that everyone has the opportunity to know the glory of golf as it is in Heaven, and can be on Earth...'

The Golden Rule

It was like hitting one of those big concrete tee markers stuck in the ground with a long spike. My hands stung from the impact. The ball was bolted to the green.

"You wouldn't listen, would you? Had to see if you could do it. After all we've been through all you can think about is beating The Pro... Have you forgotten the Nine Commandments already?"

I had had just about enough. And I decided it was time to tell him so.

"You must think I'm really out to lunch. Forgotten, huh? The Nine Commandments of Golf," I announced, then added with a large dose of reverent sarcasm, "According to The Pro Upstairs. One: Good golf is like good sex. The more you can feel that moment divine, the better it is. Two: It's not how many, it's *how*. Three: The minute you think *you've* got golf — it's got *you*. Four: Your imagination is your preview of golf's coming attractions. Five: Golf treats everyone the same. Except for those who don't believe it — who usually get what they deserve. Six: Expect the worst and you'll rarely be disappointed. Expect the best and you may surprise yourself. Seven: To play your best golf it helps to be out of your mind! Eight: Learn to enjoy the time in between — there's so much of it. And Nine: Golf is happiness!! Right?"

"Well done."

"And not one of them says anything about not wanting to beat the hell out of whoever you're playing with!!!"

"Whomever."

"Who cares!"

"You know, I think you are ready."

"For what?"

"The Golden Rule. But before I give it to you, I want to make you a deal."

"What kind of a deal?" I asked hesitantly.

"If I promise to let you go for that putt with the possibility that you may make it and beat me, you have to promise me something first."

"Like what?"

"You will share these Commandments with golfers all over your Earth. Somehow, some way, you will see that these secrets for mastering the game are spread among the people so that everyone has the opportunity to know the glory of golf as it is in Heaven, and can be on Earth..."

As The Pro continued to speak, his face began to change. I swear I saw the tips of horns starting to sprout from the sides of hs head. And his eyebrows twisted into that of Satan himself...

"...If you do not do this, your memory of this entire evening will be stripped away and you will suffer a nightmare of everlasting misfortune and misery on the golf course for the rest of your days in this life and the next!"

I wanted to run, or wake up — anything to get away!

"Good..." he said, "I knew you'd see it my way."

Then, just as suddenly, his face changed back to The Pro Upstairs I knew.

"Good... I knew you'd see it my way."

"So here it is. The Golden Rule of Golf. Get this and all the rest will be as easy as... sliding down the razor blade of life."

I felt a twinge from my spikes up to what was left of my mind.

"Ever heard the phrase, 'Today is the first day of the rest of your life'?"

I nodded.

"You Earthlings really made a big thing about it a few years ago. But as usual you got it screwed up. What if today was the *last* day of your life? Now that's the way to approach the game of golf!"

"What a horrible thought!" I gasped.

"Not at all. In fact, it's the Golden Rule: Play each round as if it was the last golf you will ever play! Just imagine what it would be like if you teed it up on number one knowing it was going to be your last round of golf. That after today, your clubs would be sold for scrap iron, and you couldn't go to a golf tournament or even watch one on television. That you'd never again be allowed to bury yourself in the pages of a golf magazine; that you could never drive by a golf course, or smell the fresh mowed fairways from around the next bend. Imagine that after this one last round, your relationship with golf is over, finished, cut off at the hosel, dead."

A chill swept over me and I began to feel dizzy and sick.

"So the question is, how would you play this last round? How many clubs would you break if you hit a couple out of bounds or missed a two-foot putt? What kind of score do you think you'd shoot if this was your last round? Would you get crazy if you didn't break 100? Or 90? Or 80?? Would it even matter if you beat your Pro?? Or would there be something else going on inside that was alive to things other than your score? The very act of swinging the club and feeling the ball take off in flight would be something to enjoy and experience to the utmost. All right, so maybe the ball came up a little short and even found the sand trap in front of the green. But since this is your

"Play each round as if it was the last golf you will every play!"

last round, you might have a whole different attitude about being in the sand. You might even be glad to be there. I mean, if you don't hit any more shots in traps for the rest of the day, this could be your last chance to feel the clubhead slide through the grains of sand running out on this last go 'round at the game. You might even take your shoes off and wiggle your feet to see how the sand feels from the bottom of your soles. Or maybe you'll really hang one out there and find a water hazard. 'Hey! I'm in the drink... Are you kidding? Of course I'm going to play it! This may be my last chance.' Even walking from shot to shot would be exciting. Your senses would be alive to the soft, lush fairways under foot. The breeze in your face cooling the sun at your back would be pure ecstasy. Would you spend these last moments worried about having to play the next three holes into the wind instead of downwind?"

"Let it blow?" came roaring out of me.

"If this was your last round of golf, the time in between shots would be filled with wonderful memories of your best golf from the past. You'd be filled with visions of striding down the magnificent fairways of the beautiful places golf brought into your life. You would drink it all in with senses alive to the experience of simply being on a golf course. And those 80 or 100 shots taking up less than three minutes during this last round? How fast would you really want to get each one over with? Would you 'miss 'em quick,' or try to enjoy every millisecond of the act, giving yourself up to the golf swing however it happens and wherever it takes you?"

"Take me. Take me!" I implored, completely under his spell.

"This last round of golf would probably be the most enjoyable round you ever played. So why not make your next round your last! And the one after that, your last again! It's all there waiting for you — fantasy fulfillment, imagination, the time in between, the moment divine — you can have it all if you simply play golf as if it's the last

> **'** *His sparkling eyes and loving smile made my Earthbound desires seem selfish and unimportant — at least in the cosmic scheme of things.* **'**

golf you will ever play."

The Pro and I stood silent for a long moment.

"You know, Sport, these Commandments are only secrets because so few people put them to use. Truth is, they've been around since the beginning of time. Just seem to have gotten lost in the rough along the way. In fact, 4,500 years ago there was something written in Sanskrit that says it all...

'Look well to this one day, for it and it alone is life. In the brief course of this one day lie all the verities and realities of your existence; the pride of growth, the glory of action, the splendor of beauty. Yesterday is only a dream and tomorrow is but a vision. Yet each today, well lived, makes every yesterday a dream of happiness and each tomorrow a vision of hope. Look well, therefore, to this one day, for it, and it alone, is life!' "

His sparkling eyes and loving smile made my Earthbound desires seem selfish and unimportant — at least in the cosmic scheme of things. Then he gave me that Tom Selleck eyebrow bounce and said:

"Go ahead, Sport. Knock it in."

He meant it too.

At this point I was too wrung out to care whether I made it or not. But after the big deal I had made, I wasn't about to pick it up and say forget it. Besides, deep down in my spike-marked soul I still wanted to make it. To beat The Pro Upstairs.

I marked and lifted my ball to clean it, then placed it back on the spot. I took a deep breath, then stroked it toward the hole. Halfway there I felt it was in. A foot from the hole I knew I had made it. I watched as it rolled to the very edge of the cup...

The Putt

"Oh, my God! I'm sorry!" rang in my head. A man was running towards me.

"I'm really sorry. I didn't know anybody was over here or I would have yelled. Are you all right?"

"Yeah... I think so," I said. I was flat on my back. Pushing myself up into a sitting position, I reached to my forehead and felt a sore spot right between my eyes.

"God, I'm sorry. I've never sliced one that bad before. I figured this late in the afternoon on Christmas Eve, nobody'd be out here."

I looked around slowly. I was back on the 12th tee. And the man talking to me was not The Pro Upstairs.

"You didn't happen to see anyone else around here, did you?"

"No."

"A little guy. Dressed sorta funny... Eyebrows like Magnum P.I.? Hair like Einstein?"

"Mmmm... maybe I better help you back to the clubhouse. Take you over to emergency."

"No. I'm fine. Really..." Then I remembered. My driver. I had thrown it into that tree. And it had been thrown right back and nailed me in the head.

"You see a club laying around here? A driver?" I asked.

"No. Nothing around here."

I got to my feet and headed straight for the tree.

"Wait a minute. Where are you going? You shouldn't be —"

"I'm fine. Thanks. See ya around..." I said, wanting him to leave. I had to find out. I got to the base of the tree and looked up.

There it was. Hanging from a branch about half way up. I shook some of the lower branches, jarring things above just enough so that my old MT driver came falling down, landing harmlessly at my feet.

And then realization began to set in...

It never happened. The whole thing never happened. It was all a dream. I didn't want to believe it, but the truth was evident. My club never came flying back at me. Some guy's ball did, and that's what knocked me out.

There was no Pro Upstairs or anything else. I imagined the whole thing.

Imagination. There was something about imagination The Pro had told me. Something...

What was it?

I couldn't remember. Maybe I should see a doctor. My head was feeling a little fuzzy...

It was definitely time to pack it in and get home in time for Christmas Eve with my wife.

I slid my driver back in my bag, slung the thing over my shoulder and headed across the bridge over the Carmel River back towards the clubhouse.

Then something strange happened.

As I started to head back up the 10th hole something told me I didn't want to do that. It wasn't so much a voice as a feeling, a force beckoning me to turn left, away from the clubhouse and towards the 14th hole.

I found myself not even wanting to argue or fight the desire and began walking towards the 14th tee. I didn't know why I was doing this or what was in store for me. It just felt... right.

I didn't even have the desire to hit a ball off the 14th tee. Now that was weird. Give me an open hole and I'm always ready to hit a couple of shots. But I didn't want to. Somehow, I sensed, it wasn't what I was there for.

Then what was?

I didn't know, but whatever it was made me want to get to it. I began to walk faster. Without realizing it I found myself humming...

"Zip-a-dee-do-dah, zip-a-dee-a..."

Where did that come from? I hadn't heard or thought about that song in years. And yet I found myself singing and strutting down the 14th fairway like Brae'r Rabbit himself!

Without missing a beat I marched through the 14th fairway and straight ahead onto the 15th.

A putt! It was coming back. I was on the 15th green with... The Pro Upstairs. That's it! If I made my putt, I'd beat him.

Sure, it was only a dream. But I had to finish it. I had to know.

As I reached the 15th green, the sky was beginning to fill with the red of a spectacular Christmas sunset. I dropped a ball, took one practice stroke, set up, and hit it.

It never had a chance. The ball was to the right from the start. Halfway there it was still way too far right.

A foot from the hole it was still to the right. Then it happened...

The ball began to break left. Hard left. Impossible! Everything goes to the right from that angle. It can't go left! It simply can't!!

But it did. And it broke straight into the heart of the hole.

I stood there completely stunned as the most glorious sunset washed over me.

"There is no way on this Earth that ball can go left from there."

The words were barely out when I had to smile. Of course I was right. There was no way on this Earth... But maybe, just maybe, I was dealing with something not of this small planet. Something strange and wonderful...

Epilogue

The rest of Christams Eve was spent in a more traditional fashion with my wife's folks coming over to our place for dinner. I dutifully explained to all that the prominent red bump in the middle of my forehead wasn't serious, but just one of the hazards that went with the territory of playing perhaps one hole too many on Christmas Eve.

As usual, we traded a few harmless jokes about my love for the game — family obligations notwithstanding — and a couple of times I was even tempted to tell them about my experience. Rather my dream. Or whatever it was. Just the fact that I wasn't sure what it was kept me quiet. And one other thing.

I couldn't remember enough. Which wasn't like me. I always remember my dreams. Well, maybe not always. But most of the time I do. Certainly the good ones.

Except this time it was all in fragments. Nothing seemed to fit. There was this funny looking old golf pro. We had played a few holes together. And when I made that putt on the 15th, I knew I had beaten him.

But there was more to it than that. I knew it. I had this terrible feeling I had made some pact, a promise... But what?

My mind was not into the Christmas Eve festivities. Fortunately it was not hard to feign a headache and excuse myself early to go to bed and recover from my hit in the head.

The family was very understanding and expressed hope I'd feel better in the morning.

The truth is, I thought that if I could get to sleep, maybe I could get back into this dream and find out what I had promised to do.

It was the longest night of my life. I couldn't get to sleep — much less work up my dream. The harder I tried to relax and nod off, the more my mind kept searching for words that would unlock the answers for me.

By Christmas morning I was worn out.

I sat on the couch as Barbara played Santa Claus and handed out the presents from under the tree.

I was trying to enjoy the proceedings, but my mind was still haunted by the horrible feeling that I had forgotten something terribly important. Something that could change the course of the lives of millions of people. Something that only I could do...

Fortunately my wife is used to my mind being off in strange places. Whenever I'm working on a new book, she knows that just because we're in the same room together and she's talking to me doesn't necessarily mean I'm really there.

"Now that's strange," I heard Barbara say. "There's no tag on this one. I don't even remember putting it under the tree. Unless... Is this one of your little surprises, honey?"

"Huh?" I really hadn't been listening.

"This present. There's no name on it. Is it for me?" she asked, smiling.

"I don't know. Go ahead and open it." I told her.

Barbara pulled the paper off the box and immediately frowned.

"Golf balls. More golf balls! You need more golf balls like you need a hole in the head."

"Which I already have, thank you very much."

"I'm sorry... Now that's strange. Don't they usually come in dozens?"

"Usually..." I answered, without really thinking about it.

"Well, there's only nine."

It took about three seconds and then it hit me like my MT driver between the eyes.

"NINE!" I yelped, catapulted off the couch and dove at my wife who screamed.

"What's wrong?! What happened!?"

"Nothing. Nothing is wrong! Everything is great! Wonderful... I think," I said as I grabbed the box from her and looked at one of the balls.

"My God... It happened. It really happened! They're here. They're all here!!"

"What?? What are you talking about?"

"No one is going to believe it... Hell, I don't believe it!"

"Believe what? What is it?... Let me see."

Barbara took one of the balls out of the box and read, " 'The Seventh Commandment. To play your best golf it helps to be out of your mind — The Pro Upstairs...' The Pro Upstairs??"

"Well, he used to be The Pro Downstairs. You see, honey, golf was actually the Devil's idea, with quicksand in the traps and hot coals on the tees to speed up play because it took forever..."

And I proceeded to tell her the whole story.

That was Christmas Day in 1985. I know what you're thinking. And you're right. It's taken me a few years to keep my part of the bargain and tell the story you've just read.

"Merry Christmas to all, and to all... Keep swinging!"

I'd like to think the time has given me the perspective to tell the tale of that magical Christmas Eve with more open-mindedness and understanding than would have been possible before.

To those of you who, after reading this, find yourselves asking this golfer, "You don't really believe all this metaphysical mumbo jumbo, do you?" I can only answer this way:

There are people who believe in Adam and Eve and the Garden of Eden. Folks who believe in reincarnation. People who swear to have been taken aboard UFO's. Millions of people believe in Santa Claus, Peter Pan, and E.T.

As for me... I believe in The Pro Upstairs.

And in spite of that, Barbara and I are still married. I wonder if it has anything to do with the First Commandment?

Acknowledgements

I cannot end without special thanks to some Earthlings and others, whose special contributions helped bring this story to light.

My sincerest thank you to my illustrator, Doug Goodwin, who listened to my description of The Pro Upstairs I encountered that wondrous night and brought him into the light for all to behold...

To Debbie and Liz in Carmel Valley who never laughed (at least in front of my face) as they suggested ways to set the type and make this story easy on the eyes — if not the mind.

To Layne Littlepage Maher, who gently showed me the error of my grammatical ways and suggested how I might better bring the events of my memory to life on the page.

To the wisdom of Michael Murphy, Timothy Gallwey, Norman Cousins, Wayne Dyer and especially Eykis. Long live Eykis!

A special thank you to Jim Langley, a golf professional who has always lived and shared the glory of golf, even before his own "close encounter" with The Pro Upstairs.

And loving thanks to my wife, Barbara, who inspired, encouraged, and finally begged me to tell the story you've just read — no doubt so SHE wouldn't have to hear it anymore!

And finally to The Pro Upstairs — there for all of us, if we but open our eyes, our minds and our hearts.

OTHER GOLF BOOKS BY MARK OMAN

The Sensuous Golfer — How To Play The Game... On The Course And Off!
Illustrated by Tom Nix
(72 pages—32 illustrations) ISBN 0-917346-01-7 $6.95

Whether you keep it in your bag or under your bed, this book will put you in position to play around with the best of 'em!

"The perfect gift for the passionate player who has all the equipment — but doesn't know what to do with it!"

Joan Rivers

How To Live With A Golfaholic—A Survival Guide for Family and Friends of Passionate Players
Illustrated by Jay Campbell and Carl Christ
(96 pages—20 illustrations) ISBN 0-917346-14-9 $6.95

The only book to help you survive the traps and hazards of a golfer's magnificent obsession.

"Mark Oman's observations are all in the birdie circle."

Charles M. Schulz

Portrait Of A Golfaholic
Illustrated by Gary Patterson
(96 pages—30 illustrations) ISBN 0-8092-5335-6 $6.95

The bible of Golfaholics Anonymous. A look into the wide world of golfaholism.

"A great gift to the guy in your foursome who is always pressing for 6 A.M. tee times... Every sinner loves company."

Los Angeles Times